MW01118901

I, Shrink

Ichabod Green M.D.

Cover Art by
Don Sinish

To Marsha & Roger
Harold Zeckel M.D.
aka Ichabod Green

Example isn't another way to teach,
it is the only way to teach
– Albert Einstein

$\mathcal{A}$CKNOWLEDGEMENTS

I thank all my patients as I learned so much from them, and I would like to thank all my therapists and everyone else who encouraged me to write this book.

About 20 years ago, my son-in-law, who was teaching psychology, asked me for examples of patients whom I had treated. I wrote him a letter about five cases. He read my letter to his class and wrote me saying that I should write a book about my experiences as a psychiatrist. What follows is that book.

SHORT TERM CASES

■ #1 ████████████████████████████

A young lady came to see me because she was unable to have orgasms when having sex. She said her boyfriends always wanted to know whether she had had one. She felt like this was a pressure on her to orgasm. She said that it would be like their orgasm, not hers. She asked me whether I could help her; I told her I didn't know but maybe if we talked more, what was interfering would become clear. While taking the family history, she mentioned that it made her angry that her mother always seemed to take credit for her achievements. Some sessions after, she related a dream in which she was a dishrag which her mother was waving around. I felt the meaning of the dream was clear enough so that it required no interpretation. She felt like a dishrag and dishrags don't have orgasms. Then one day she came to my office wearing a see-through blouse. (this was not unusual in those first years of Women's Lib). I didn't know what to say, but I remembered reading that a well-known psychiatrist said to his female patient who was sitting across from him in a revealing way, "Are you trying to seduce me?" So I thought I should do the same. After remarking about her blouse, I asked my patient, "Are you trying to seduce me?" In the most innocent, shocked tone of voice she replied, "No Dr. Green ! Why would you ask me such a thing?" I felt like disappearing into my chair like I had said the wrong thing. "Bad psychiatrist!" I admonished myself. Not long after that she came in telling me that she had had an orgasm during sex for the first time. I intentionally said to her, "**you must be very happy about that**", making sure that the credit belonged to her. Not long after that she told me that she no longer needed therapy. Although I never heard, I assume that she went on to enjoy many blissful sexual experiences.

Looking back on it I asked myself did my asking whether she was trying to seduce me - implying that she was sexually attractive - actually help her? I will never know, however, I came to believe over time that nonverbal messages are often more convincing to the emotional mind than intellectual interpretations. I saw this young lady early on in my practice so I didn't know whether this was a common reason for seeking therapy. However, I did, many years later, see a young woman who told me she was no longer having orgasms with her boyfriend. It turned out to be merely an indicator of the relationship's disintegration. As for how I reacted to women speaking about their intimate sexual feelings and behavior, I felt complimented that they trusted me enough to discuss such things with me.

I should mention here that I saw a lady in her 60's who was complaining of her knees aching at night such that it interfered with her sleep. During the sessions which followed, she spoke at length of being ashamed of her promiscuous sexual behavior when she was a teenager, feeling she, therefore, could not take credit for the high esteem in which people generally held her. I asked her to describe her knee pain. Apparently it had nothing to do with how much exercise she had had that day, nor was there any tenderness, swelling, or redness of the knee joints. I said to her that the symptom sounded as if it were psychological. She thought about that and it suddenly it dawned on her that it was an expression of her shame and wish that she had kept her legs together when she was in her teens. Upon discovering this, the symptom mostly disappeared. (Of course, this was only one of numerous symptoms, but I was surprised at how effective her becoming aware of the connection was.)

■ #2 ▬▬▬▬▬▬▬▬▬▬▬▬▬▬▬▬▬▬▬▬▬▬▬▬▬

Mr. Jones was a married man in his late 30s who came to me complaining of anxiety. He had grown up on a farm in Europe and as he was the oldest son, he was slated to inherit the farm. However, he would not be able to marry his sweetheart until the farm was his, and he didn't want to wait to marry her until he was in his 40s. So he and his sweetheart moved to the United States and got married. While exploring his history, he told me that his father would never allow him to run the tractor or other farm machinery despite the fact that all his friends were allowed to. Pleading with his father never did any good. His father just didn't have faith in him.

Once here in the U.S., he went to work in the then fledgling computer industry. At that time computers consisted of a tangle of wires in the back of the box going every which way, looking much like the old telephone switchboards. Personal computers were still unknown, but all the colleges and universities had them for student and faculty use. Every now and then one of the computers would develop a bug and he worked at fixing the problem. He was the type of person who wouldn't give up until he had it fixed, even if it meant staying up 48 hours or more. Because of this his employers relied heavily on him, and they would call on him when others had failed. So he rose up the ranks to become the person of last resort responsible for all his company's computers on the eastern seaboard. Then, after being away from his homeland for ten years, he decided he wanted to visit his parents at the old farm. When he came back to see me after that vacation, he told me that during his visit he noticed a broken light switch in the house. He said to his father, "Let me fix that", to which his father replied, "Oh no, you can't do that", and wouldn't let him even touch it. Upon relating this during our session, he experienced a terrible anxiety attack and fell to the floor in front of me.

A few visits after that he told me he felt he no longer needed therapy as now he could handle his anxiety himself. And so the sessions came to an end. I never heard from him again.

A number of reflections came to me about this case. First of all, I never interpreted anything for this patient; he did all the work himself. I even thought that if I had tried to make interpretations, it might have sent a message to him that he wasn't capable of doing the work by himself. Secondly, it reminded me that the words 'anger' and 'anxiety' both stem from the Greek, meaning 'narrow' or 'compressed'. Freud attributed anxiety to repressed anger. Over the years, it became obvious to me that unresolved anger is behind many mental problems. This case again illustrates that the goal of therapy is to make the unconscious conscious, and when the patient is convinced that these are what is determining the symptom, then the patient has control over it. As long as the feeling seems to be coming from nowhere, then the patient feels helpless against it. As for this patient's falling on the floor in front of me during an anxiety attack, I took this simply as an indication of how powerful his anxiety was, and that it was my job to sit with patients during the expression of powerful feelings, sending the message that these feelings were not destructive to me.

#3

A young lady in her 20s came to see me because she wanted to find out why she was eating compulsively. She was engaged to be married and was living with her girlfriend. She was getting fat which she was unhappy about, although she said her fiancé was not bothered by it and told her he loved her no matter what.

Right after the first visit she said she was controlling her eating better; symptomatic improvement often occurs when beginning therapy but it usually doesn't last. As usual her compulsion soon returned to its former level. We continued talking about her compulsive eating and difficulty controlling it. Then in one session she told me that when she went food shopping, she would buy two of everything so that the cashier would think she was shopping for another person also. After which she would return to her apartment and wait until her roommate was asleep, when she would eat it all herself. I thought to myself, "She is sneaking her overeating" and I said to her, "you're sneaking when your'e eating makes me think there must be something sexual about it". Suddenly she shifted to talking about her parents divorcing when she was 15. At that time one summer her father took her on a summer vacation to an island off the coast of Maine. There were lots of single parents and their children there. At night all the single adults were bed hopping and the adolescent children were doing the same. Telling me about this made her realize that she was trying to make herself unattractive. She was afraid if she were slim, other young men would hit on her and she might give in as she had carried around the "Sure, why not?" attitude since she was 15. As she didn't want to cheat on her fiancé, she then realized she could say "No" and therefore she would no longer need to eat compulsively to make herself undesirable.

She had gotten the answer to her question and so didn't need therapy anymore. She said, "Thank you" and "Good-bye" and I never heard from her again. Before therapy she was unaware of the connection between the root of her giving-in attitude and her compulsion to overeat.

It was always gratifying to me when something came up which caused a sudden, seemingly unrelated, association to arise which turned out to be crucial.

#4

A college coed came to see me because she was feeling nauseated all the time. Her doctor felt the problem was psychological and referred her to me. I asked her about her life. She told me that before she came to college, she had to take care of her alcoholic father as her mother wasn't around. At times she had to bathe her drunken father and sometimes she had to call an ambulance because he would vomit blood. She had gotten away from him by coming to the university as her home was distant.

At the time she was in a difficult relationship with a boyfriend who was both a drinker and gambler. She said she never knew whether he would return to the apartment that night. I listened patiently as she told me how frustrated she was with the relationship. After listening to her going on about this for some time, I said to her, "I don't see how you stand it !" Shortly after that, she decided to break up with that boyfriend. I recall the scene when she was saying Good-bye to him. Both of them were crying when she told him she had to leave. It was obvious that despite how much his behavior upset her, they genuinely loved each other.

Not long after that she met another young man. She seemed very happy with him; he hardly drank at all. Her complaint of feeling nauseated had apparently vanished afterwards as time went by. Soon after meeting the new boyfriend, she told me she felt she no longer needed therapy and we terminated the sessions.

A couple of years later she sent me a letter saying she thought I probably rarely heard from patients after the therapy ended, but she wanted to let me know that she had married the last boyfriend and that they were very happy together. They had bought a farm in New Hampshire and were running it together. She finished the letter by saying that what had made the difference was when I said, "I don't see how you stand it". That made her realize that even though she loved that boyfriend (and her father), she couldn't continue to live with him (nor her father).

In this case we see Freud's Repetition Compulsion which is so powerful in many people. I realize that what I said to her was something that anyone else might have said, but my listening and caring enabled her to hear it. The tearful saying Good-bye was a dramatic illustration of ambivalence and how its resolution led to eradication of the symptom.

I rarely got any follow-up on patients after termination, so it was very nice to receive it this time.

███ #5 ██

A 44 year old married woman with two young children came in because of the sudden onset of anxiety. It seemed to occur especially when she was driving with her children in the back seat of the car. When I saw her, anxiety had just recently begun. Treatment with one of the minor tranquilizers (related to Valium) helped only minimally. We explored her present and past life. I asked her about her age and whether it meant anything particular to her. She was not really concerned about aging, but she told me that her mother had died at the age she is now. I found that unusual and asked her about the circumstances. She told me that when she was 16 and her mother was 44, they were standing in the kitchen when suddenly her mother complained of a terrible headache. It was so bad that my patient had to call for an ambulance. As they were carrying her mother out on a stretcher, her mother turned to her and said, "I think I burst a blood vessel in my head". Indeed her mother was right and she died the next day of a ruptured aneurysm in her brain. After my patient related this history to me, she realized that she was afraid that this would happen to her as she had just turned that same age. And, she realized she was afraid the same thing would happen to her when she was driving with her children in the car. Becoming aware of what was behind her anxiety enabled her to control the fear. This ended her need for therapy, after a minimum number of visits.

In this case I eventually got some follow up. Most people don't write me a letter as to how they are doing like the college student. However, many years later this lady was talking to one of her neighbors who happened to be a psychologist I worked with. My name came up, so my patient expressed to my coworker how grateful she was for my help all those years ago. As with so many patients, she really did all the work, but she gave me the credit.

Which reminds me of the time in medical school when I delivered a baby for the first time. The labor had begun prematurely and I was scrubbing up for the delivery when the baby came so quickly that the nurse actually delivered it. Even though I felt ashamed of not being there at the critical time, the patient gave me all the credit. My colleagues and I often said that we accept the credit for good results and refuse to take the blame for any bad results. Not really true as we do feel bad if a patient has bad results.

■ #6 ▬▬▬▬▬▬▬▬▬▬▬▬▬▬▬▬▬▬▬▬▬▬▬▬▬▬▬▬

A professor in his late 30s came to me because of depression. He was married and they had one child, but their second child had died shortly after childbirth. He could not seem to get over the death of this child even though more than a year had passed. He was a very soft spoken and unassuming person which did not befit someone of his status. Apparently his students and colleagues were fond of him, and some of them even used to confide their personal problems in him. He had a good marriage and their son was doing well.

After some sessions, he told me that he was born with an abnormality of his penis which had to be surgically corrected. As a result, when he matured his penis never grew to be normal in size. He spoke of how he avoided going into the shower rooms at school because the other boys would make fun of his small penis. He also avoided dating when in his teens and early 20s because he felt too insecure about sex. He was painfully envious of the other young men going out on dates. Then one day he met the woman whom he later married. He said he knew he didn't have to be afraid with her. They have been very happy together since and their sex life is mutually satisfying.

He also spoke about his father who was a laborer who wanted his sons to be "rough and tough". His two brothers were strapping young men and met with the father's expectations. The professor who was a small man seemed to be a disappointment to his father. In more ways than one he didn't seem to measure up.

I went to the medical library to find out what the normal distribution of penis size is and indeed he was at the lower end of the spectrum. In therapy I acknowledged his feelings of inferiority but I reminded him that intellectually he was superior to his father and brothers. And also that his genital size did not interfere with him and his wife's relationship in any way, while in general about half the marriages in the U.S. end in divorce. I added that many women don't care about men's penis size and in fact don't even pay attention to it. Despite the fact that one often hears "Size matters", I said penis size appeared to me to be more of a male than female preoccupation. And I assured him that the size of his penis was in no way related to the fact that his second child hadn't survived.

He and his wife mourned the death of the second child together. His waves of depression and sense of inadequacy seemed to fade, and by the end of therapy, he was able to accept himself the way he was. He was able to balance his superior qualities against his inferiorities. I eventually learned that a most significant goal of therapy is to learn to accept oneself realistically. Trying to deny one's bad feelings about oneself doesn't work as you can't fool yourself.

 #7

A young married woman in her late 20s was admitted to the psych ward because she had a terrible headache for which the doctors could find no effective treatment. I recall her walking around the ward with a towel wrapped around her head with an expression on her face as if there were a terrible weight in her head just above her eyes. Asking her about her marriage, she replied that there were no problems there. However, the nursing staff all remarked about how nasty her husband was. And when I spoke with him on the phone, I had to agree.

After she had been on our unit for a couple of weeks with no change in her headaches, despite our having tried all the medications at our disposal, we requested a neurological consultation. We transferred her to the neurology service as the neurologist had suggested. While on his service she was tried on various esoteric medications also to no avail. So he transferred her back to the psych service. The minute she reappeared on our service she announced that she had decided to divorce her husband. Simultaneously her headache vanished completely. Her husband had apparently been her headache. Over the years I saw many examples of where denial led to physical symptoms.

#8

A man in his 50s was told by his doctor that he had terminal lung cancer. In the office, the doctor told the man and his wife that he could offer no treatment. The couple were very angry about this and decided to go to the most prestigious hospital in town for a second opinion. There he was offered experimental chemotherapy. He also decided that he wanted to talk to someone about his impending death and so he came to me.

During the initial visits he spoke about his ex-wife and that she had actually propositioned their adolescent sons. This was something I had never heard before (except in jokes). Apparently the boys, to their credit, simply ignored her. After going off on this subject for a while, he began talking at length about his days in the Navy. He had manned the cannons on a destroyer during World War II. He described how they had used analog computers at that time to direct the cannons. It was clear that he enjoyed reminiscing about these days during the war.

After I had been seeing him for 3 or 4 months, his present wife called to tell me that he had died. She said that right after getting out of bed in the morning he passed out and never regained consciousness. He had died peacefully recounting a part of his life of which he was very proud. Over the years I saw many people approaching death and never noticed the stages Elizabeth Kubler Ross wrote about. It appeared to me that denial was the most common way people dealt with their approaching death. I had heard stories of people running off to some remote part of the world upon receiving a death sentence but never saw that first hand. It also seemed to me that the devoutly religious people approached death with equanimity. Would that when my time comes, I would have such faith.

I also found myself thinking that pain and suffering would be helpful, as then one would long for the end instead of being terrified.

#9

A professor in his 60s came in feeling terrible because he thought he had killed his wife. She had been in the hospital dying of cancer when she asked him to bring her a couple of glasses of orange juice. Shortly after drinking the juice she passed away. It suddenly struck him that possibly the calcium in the juice had raised her blood calcium level to where it had stopped her heart, thus blaming his actions for her death. He went to a couple of doctors telling them what he feared and they reassured him that the orange juice had not caused her death. But he was not satisfied.

I listened to him not knowing what to say. However, on the way home that evening I became curious about how much two glasses of orange juice would raise one's blood calcium level. So I looked up the number of milligrams in two large glasses of orange juice. Then I looked up the upper normal calcium level in the blood, plus looking up the normal blood volume in a small person. Adding the number of milligrams in the orange juice to the blood volume I easily calculated by how much the blood calcium concentration would be increased. I found that it wouldn't, even closely, raise the blood calcium concentration to toxic levels.

I sent a letter to the professor showing him my calculations proving that her drinking two glasses of orange juice could not have raised her calcium level to where it would have any effect on the heart. I never heard anything from him after that and I feel certain that if he showed my letter to his doctor, his doctor would have to agree with my calculations.

■ #10

A single young woman in her 20s was admitted to the psychiatric unit for the 4th time in a year because of persistent stomach pain. She was saying she wanted to kill herself because of the pain. During her stay she volunteered very little information to the staff or to me in our one-to-one sessions. As usual she said her stomach pain was worse than ever and she felt like killing herself. Somewhat reassuring to me was the fact that she said the suicidal thoughts frightened her. In one session she said that her mother was always saying to her, "Don't speak to me in that tone of voice". To me she said, " I would have changed my tone of voice if I knew what she wanted". I met with her mother who clearly loved her daughter and was trying to do the right thing. My patient hated herself and thought of herself as ugly and stupid, neither of which was true. After a few weeks she confided that she had been raped when she was 12 years old. She did say that she felt guilty about it, but she refused to go into any details. In the ensuing sessions she said her pain was getting worse and worse and she was becoming more and more disgusted. She began accusing me of not helping her and saying things like, "You don't know what to do with me, do you?", "You don't have anything to say, do you?", and "Why don't you transfer me to another psychiatrist?" I ignored her provocations and refused to transfer her. When I insisted that she continue to come to see me after she left the hospital, she said angrily that she would not. Finally she said she wanted to stay in the hospital until her $160,000 life-time insurance benefit ran out. After a while, I felt she had been in the hospital long enough and because she still spoke of wanting to hang herself, I decided to commit her to the State Hospital. I had seen very difficult patients get better when they were confronted with what it would be like at the end of the line, namely, at the State Hospital. Being confronted with unpleasant reality often makes people think twice. I later heard that they had allowed her to sign out against medical advice. I imagine that she told them she was no longer suicidal in order to be let out. When I telephoned her at home and she heard it was me, she slammed down the phone. Then I called and spoke to her mother, who, to my surprise, told me, "She is really doing very well!"

I had been told by my instructors, "If you expect gratitude, don't go into this field". Secondly I felt my sending her to the looney bin was seen by her unconscious as a symbolic reenactment of her rape. Thus her expressing her anger at me helped her get some of the anger about the rape out of her system. I believe that Freud and others refer to this as 'abreaction'. And I felt that as long as she was better, that was all that mattered .

As for how I felt about her expressing angry feelings to me, I seemed to notice over time that when patients expressed anger at me it resulted in their getting better. However, contrary to some of my colleagues, I did not try to induce patients' anger. I preferred to have it occur naturally. A couple of adolescents whom I treated in the hospital repeatedly told me how worthless they thought I was; but when it came time for them to leave the hospital, I suddenly became their best friend. The nurses often asked me how I could stand it when those patients told me to f—- myself. I didn't let it get to me. Displacement of anger is occasionally the only outlet people have. I believe it is no mere coincidence that the word 'mad' means both crazy and angry.

■ ▎ #11 ▉▉▉▉▉▉▉▉▉▉▉▉▉▉▉▉▉▉▉▉▉▉▉▉▉▉▉▉▉

A man in his early 30s who had a heart attack was told by his physician that he had a genetic abnormality of cholesterol metabolism which rendered him vulnerable to having another heart attack at any time and that the next heart attack would probably kill him. At the time there were no effective cholesterol lowering agents and diet was of limited help. The doctor said he could not predict how long this man had to live.

His wife became depressed over the prospect of losing her husband unpredictably. She was the one who sought therapy. Before she came to see me another psychiatrist had administered shock treatment, but it had little effect on her depression. After that she was referred to me.

She had lost both of her parents when she was between 11 and 12 years old. The impending death of her husband was compounding her fear of losing those whom she loved. During the therapy she expressed her feelings of worry and depression. They had two young children who were going to be subjected to the same sort of trauma she herself had experienced. I could not offer her any hope about her husband's condition; the therapy went on for about 6 months. After that length of time expressing her painful feelings, I decided to tell her that these feelings were interfering with her and her husbands' enjoying whatever time they had left together. By then she seemed able to hear it, and so she agreed and decided to act accordingly. Consequently soon afterwards, she felt that she could discontinue our sessions.

I didn't see her again until about 6 years later when she came in and told me that her husband had had another heart attack and died. She came to see me for a few sessions but it was clear to both of us that she was able to manage her emotions.

Another 6 years went by when she came to me again and told me that she had been diagnosed with terminal lung cancer. She seemed to be dealing with her own impending death and shortly afterwards she died. By that time both of the children were teenagers. They each came to talk with me after their mother's death. I felt they were dealing with the situation as well as could be expected. I never heard from either of them again.

Being a close witness to this tragic story reminded me of the fact that life is not fair. My feeling is that as a therapist it is important to simply be there and listen to the painful feelings for as long as needed. When the right time comes one can gently offer simple advice.

■ #12

Another lady in her early 30s came in complaining of terrible anxiety which began when she and her husband were divorcing. Two things she told me a number of times which stand out in my memory: 1) that the anxiety was so bad that she would rather have had cancer, and 2) that her friends could not understand why she was seeing a psychiatrist as they felt she was perfectly normal. But with me, she spoke of being extremely afraid of what was going to happen to her. I took Bill Glasser's (Reality Therapy) approach and told her she just had to keep coming and talking about her feelings. I implied that this would eventually help. After about 6 months of listening to her anguish, the severity of her anxiety finally eased and she felt she was able to go on without therapy.

About 20 years later I bumped into her at the town library. She told me that she was doing well. Because of where we were, I couldn't ask her whether she had remarried.

Her receiving supportive treatment struck me as analogous to the treatment of Rabies. The victim can survive by just supporting the functioning of the vital organs until the immune system mobilizes its forces so it can fight off the virus. In this lady's treatment the emotional support eventually enabled her own defenses to take over. Much of medical treatment depends on the body's ability to mobilize its own defenses. No less so with the mind.

A lady in her early 40s came to see me because of depression. She had had Rheumatic Fever when she was 10 and was left with Rheumatic Heart Disease as a result. The doctors told her and her parents that she probably would not live past age 40. They said her condition would eventually lead to heart failure which could not be well treated at that time. She responded to this prognosis by pushing herself to be very active and to not permit herself to be a cardiac cripple; she had decided she would face whatever happened when she reached her 40s. As part of pushing herself to be active, she became the family entertainer who hosted all the family celebrations. She continued doing this for many years so the extended family came to expect that she would always host the parties. They depended on her.

Now about 30 years after her receiving her diagnosis as a child, the treatment for heart failure had improved such that she would be able to live to a normal old age using medications. As a result she became depressed! The opposite of what one would expect. She found that now she no longer wanted to push herself to do all the entertaining and instead wanted to relax. What made her depressed was realizing that she would have to refuse to take on these responsibilities and would have to let everyone know she would no longer do so. After her relatively brief course of therapy, she decided what she wanted to do and she would have to face everyone in the family. Her depression simply evaporated.

We were taught, which, I think Freud believed due to his experimenting with cocaine, that medication simply masked the symptoms and did not eradicate of the cause of the symptom. With medication alone, this lady might still be pushing herself and wondering why she felt depressed and compelled to continue being the entertainer.

■ #14 ▰▰▰▰▰▰▰▰▰▰▰▰▰▰▰▰▰▰▰▰▰▰▰

A married man in his 30s wanted to know why he was waking up frequently each night. Together we explored his present and past life looking for clues. After some time he told me that his father, who was a policeman, would go out drinking after getting off duty before coming home. My patient would be asleep when his father returned. Many of those nights his drunken father would come home and start punching his wife. My patient related how he would wake up and jump out of bed when he heard the crack from his father's punching his mother. He would then run in to the room to try to protect her.

After growing up and marrying, he and his wife bought a house. Often in the middle of the night as the house was settling it would make a cracking sound. Upon verbalizing this, he realized that it was this cracking sound of the house settling which would suddenly wake him up. Putting two and two together he was able to resist his impulse to jump out of bed and allow himself to return to a comfortable sleep. He required no sleeping medications.

Training

As a medical student I spent one month in one of the state hospitals. Although we had heard lectures, we hadn't seen any patients yet until I was assigned to see one of the female patients at the State Hospital. She was married and in her thirties. She had a delusion that her body was constantly flaking off and thus gradually disintegrating. The first visit with her went fine as I asked routine questions which she answered. However, the second visit began with a few words followed by a prolonged silence. I believed in Freud's technique of 'free association' with occasionally asking what the patient was feeling or thinking. This led nowhere. Finally I thought to myself, "Psychiatrists are always interested in sex", therefore I asked her how her sex life was. Saying nothing, she immediately got up out of her chair and walked out. She refused to see me again. I certainly wasn't being a very successful psychiatrist.

After finishing medical school I chose to fulfill my two years of compulsory military duty, hoping that during that time I would be able to decide which specialty I wanted. I was assigned to an army hospital in Germany where I worked in preventive medicine plus working in the general medical clinic. When the army psychiatrist asked me whether

I wanted to work a couple of days in his clinic under his supervision, I agreed. My first patient was a beautiful married lady in her early 20s whose complaint was of a terribly disfiguring scar on her nose which she had sustained in a recent auto accident. Sitting across from her I didn't see anything, so I asked if I could take a closer look. I got up and went over to her to examine her nose, but I couldn't see any scar at all. I sat down and told her I didn't see anything abnormal, but she insisted that she had a scar there. I never did get a chance to explore her complaint further as her husband was transferred to another location shortly after.

I was also occasionally asked to evaluate soldiers for security clearances. One man surprised me by telling me that he had been a regular heroin abuser before he joined the military, but immediately upon joining the army, he stopped the heroin without experiencing any withdrawal effects at all.

While working in the psychiatric clinic, I decided that psychiatry was the specialty for me. I didn't know whether I could help anyone, but I was fascinated by listening to the patients. Thus I applied for a residency training program in Boston and was accepted.

During the first year, I worked on the psychosomatic unit of the hospital plus, under supervision, seeing patients in the outpatient clinic. One day, with a couple of the supervising psychiatrists observing, I evaluated a young lady for possible outpatient therapy. My supervisors then told me I had to take her on as my therapy patient. I said I didn't want to because I felt too uncomfortable in her presence as she was so alluring. Nevertheless, they said I had to take her on as my patient. During our sessions, sitting across from her, I squirmed in my chair while she spoke about all the things she and her boyfriend were doing in bed together. I described my sessions to my supervisor who said, "She's trying to make you jealous". It should have been my job to say to her, "Are you trying to make me jealous?", but I couldn't do it as I was afraid of the consequences. Namely, I was afraid she might respond by saying, "You know where I live. Just come over and see me some time", which, if this were to happen, I was not sure I would have been able to resist. I kept my mouth shut.

We also attended conferences in which cases were discussed by the staff. One time they presented a married man who lived with his wife in a house together with his father. When they mentioned that the father was having sex with his daughter-in-law, suddenly my head felt like it was a bell going Bong Bong and I felt like I was going to pass out. I remained in my seat closing my ears to the rest of the presentation. This way I managed to stay in the room.

I also especially recall a young man whom I was seeing for therapy, who asked me what he should do about some issue. When I said that I didn't know what he should do, he said to me, "Well if you don't know, then it is just the blind leading the blind". Inside I said to myself, "Yes, it is the blind leading the blind". I didn't yet know how to reply to such questions.

Also, I was responsible for psychiatric consultations on the medical and surgical services of the hospital. One such case was that of a young lady who had just had surgery after which she wouldn't urinate. On my way over to see her, I procrastinated, hoping the problem would resolve itself during my delay. When I arrived at the ward, the surgical resident told me that the young lady had peed after all. I breathed a sigh of relief and asked him how it happened. He told me that he asked her why she wouldn't pee. She said she couldn't, because she felt too embarrassed doing so in front of all the other people in the room. There were no other people in the room! She was actually alone there. But the resident had decided to pretend he was ushering all the people out of the room after which he left the room himself. He waited outside for a few minutes and then knocked on the door. After she let him in, she told him she had been able to urinate. I was off the hook. I thought to myself, "This surgical resident is a better psychiatrist than I am". As time went on, I was to see other examples of where non-psychologically trained people were better at handling difficult situations than I imagined I would have been.

During my second year of residency I was assigned to a women's admission unit at the State Hospital. Initially I went to the hospital in the morning afraid, not knowing what to expect. Suddenly I was to be among thirty floridly psychotic women. I unlocked the heavy oak door with one of those large old keys to let myself in, which I had to lock again behind me from the inside. The patients were milling about . They were wearing old clothes that probably had been donated by Good Will together with rubber soled shoes and socks. None of them seemed the least bit interested in her appearance. The behaviors I witnessed on this ward were often very strange. I saw a young lady walking around oblivious of her menstrual blood running down her leg, another pulled her artificial eye out of its socket and bounced it on the floor, one woman took off all her clothes just to show me a blemish on her hip, and one young woman dug a piece of feces out of her rear end and offered it to me.

One day, as I entered the ward, one of the patients came up to me furiously angry, shouting a string of verbal nonsense at me. She was so angry the spittle was flying out of her mouth as she yelled at me. I just stood there and listened. She ended her tirade by lifting her leg and letting out a loud blast of gas. I said, "Well, at least that's something". She just walked away. Upon hearing this story a fellow resident said to me, "You really understand these people". I don't think I understood them, but I did feel for them.

I particularly remember a very crazy woman in her 30s who would lie down on the floor with her arms outstretched saying she was Jesus Christ on the cross. She always talked about having lost her Oomph. One time I watched her eating in the dining hall. She would bring the spoon up to her lips but then put it back in the bowl. She did this four or five times before putting it in her mouth to swallow. One day, she said she wanted to leave the hospital. I took her downstairs pointing to the front door saying, " You may leave." Instead, she just turned around and walked back into the building. From the nurses, I learned that she had recently delivered a baby, and in the past, after each delivery, she would go completely bonkers and have to be admitted to the hospital again. She would remain on the ward for three or four months after which she would return to normal. Then her husband would come to bring her home. In between these episodes, the nurses said she was as normal as blueberry pie. That one example convinced me that Postpartum psychosis is an organic disorder. I imagined it to be due to abrupt hormonal change.

Years later in my practice, I saw an elderly lady who had suddenly developed manic episodes occurring every six months like clockwork after she had begun menopause, which had been years before I first saw her. She was said to have Involutional Melancholia. Probably hormonal, I thought.

A manic lady on the State Hospital ward, who had an artificial leg, had a reputation for escaping, only to be brought back by the police shortly after. She was well-known to the police. When I discussed her with my supervisor, he told me to take away her artificial leg so that she can't escape. Something inside me said I can't do that, but I did it. Neither she nor the other patients objected to my confiscating her leg. In fact, when Christmastime came, she and all the other patients threw a party for me giving me a card they had made.

Every weekday morning I held an hour-long group meeting for all the patients and nurses. A young lady who had a very tough demeanor once threatened me during the meeting, saying, "Dr. Green, I'm gonna kill you!" After her threatening me, I told her I could no longer see her for individual sessions because she was frightening me. She said, "Dr. Green, You know I'm just a bowl of jelly inside" That relieved my fear and we were friends after that. I had heard that her father had been murdered by the mob. She was notorious in the hospital for causing a ruckus every night so the doctor on-call had to come over late at night to straighten out the situation. She gave me a poem she had written, the first two lines of which were, "Better dead than alive, but best is to never have been born".

Her best friend on the ward was a cutter. The cuts always had to be sewn. She spoke in a monotone, or as we said "she had a flat affect". I saw this among men in the prison and always felt it to be a sign of suppressed rage. She had good reason to be full of rage. When she was little, her father used to extinguish his cigarettes on her arm. To punish her, he would hit her, and if she cried, he would hit her again because she was crying. At times he would hang her up in the clothes' closet. He and her mother would frequently leave without telling her. She would be left alone and afraid, not knowing where her parents were or if they were ever returning. My heart went out to her. When my assignment to that unit came to an end, I heard from the psychiatrist who succeeded me that she had been running around from one emergency room to another because she believed she had the clap. The doctors all told her she didn't have gonorrhea and refused to treat her. Shortly after that, she committed suicide. I went to the funeral. I couldn't believe she was really gone. Sometimes I thought I saw her walking on the street, but on looking closer, I could see it was not her. I missed her. From her, I learned that some children actually endure the most horrible childhoods you could imagine. After death, I certainly hope she rests in peace, because here on earth she had no peace of mind.

Much later, I could understand that her believing she had gonorrhea was symbolic of the terrible feelings she had about herself. No matter that it was a delusion. It was how she felt. The result of the doctors' refusals meant to her that nobody cared. Pretending to treat her gonorrhea as if it were real - like the doctor who ushered the imaginary people out of the room when the young lady refused to urinate- would have meant to her that somebody did care. I often said to myself that mental illnesses are the result of disorders of love or caring.

For the second half of the year at the state hospital, I was transferred to a men's unit for the chronically mentally ill. It had a ward of one hundred men. The average hospital stay for all one hundred was fifteen years. The men never requested to have individual sessions with me. Individual issues, such as fights, were dealt with in the nurses' office. The nurses did 90% of the work, and I merely discussed the patients' medications with the nurses. The patients all had small chores such as making their beds, sweeping the floor, etc. When it came time for their medications, they would line up at the nurses' station for what they called their "poison". I felt they actually valued their "poison", so if one of them were remiss about doing his chores, the punishment was that he couldn't get his "poison" that day. That usually worked. These patients rarely caused any problems, although one time when my supervisor told me I should lock the doors, then all of the men acted up until we decided to leave the doors open again.

Two of the chronic patients stand out in my mind. The first was a man who had killed his father. He stabbed his father to defend his mother from his father. He was very quiet, hardly ever saying a word, nor did he seem to befriend any of the other men. It seemed to me that he felt extremely contrite about what he had done, despite the fact that the court had ruled it a justified homicide.

The most terrible case was of a young man who had castrated himself. It hurts to even imagine it. Paradoxically, he strutted around as if he were a tough guy. During a family meeting with his parents, while they were sitting down, he was pacing back and forth grunting. After a bit, his father barked, "Cut it out !" at him. I asked myself why the father used this particular expression with his son. My guess was that the father subconsciously expressed his wish to emasculate his son, and I would suspect he had expressed this wish in covert ways many times. And further, I guessed the son psychotically acted out his father's wish. However, I agree, I am surmising from very little information. But it reminds me of M. Scott Peck's story about the parents who bought their son a rifle, sending the message that they wanted him to commit suicide the same way his brother had done.

At the end of the year, I asked myself whether I had done any good at all. I concluded that I mainly functioned as a stabilizing influence for the patients' restless and chaotic minds. As for understanding them, I often think of one nurse's aide, who was eating an apple and allowing one of the patients to have a bite of it. To me, that is real understanding. However, it is not something I would have done.

VIGNETTES

■ Anxiety ▊▊▊▊▊▊▊▊▊▊▊▊▊▊▊▊▊▊▊▊▊▊▊▊

What follows are vignettes of patients I saw, mostly as medication patients, that is, patients I saw for 15 minute visits once every three months.

For a number of years I saw a lady who had anxiety for which I prescribed a minor tranquilizer, which she found helpful. She was unhappy in her marriage, although she had a cheerful demeanor. She kept a clean and orderly house, but her husband was the type who would track mud into the house without making the slightest apologies. Her husband was a dour fellow who usually remained holed up in the cellar with his computer. My patient, on the contrary, was one of those ladies who would spread sunshine wherever she went. She worked as an aide in a nursing home where all the demented patients would exclaim joyfully, "Oh, here's Lily!", when she came in, whereas they didn't know the names of the other staff. Lily liked going on group excursions, while her husband, who wasn't interested in going along, would stay home. When Lily was away on those trips, entertaining everyone, she never took any of her tranquilizers. She had no withdrawal symptoms when she stopped them while away from home. When she returned home, she started right back on them. You can draw your own conclusions as to what her anxiety stemmed from.

Another lady spoke about how angry she was at her husband. But when I asked her why she stayed in the marriage, she told me that as long as she stayed married, her OCD didn't bother her. She proceeded to tell me that her OCD consisted of her feeling compelled to count all the cracks in the walls of her home. This symptom was so intolerable to her that staying with her husband was the lesser of the two evils. Often the best you can hope for with patients like this is to listen and listen until the patient becomes resigned to the fact that something like staying in the marriage is the best decision. Probably to analyze the problem more deeply would have required prolonged therapy.

Another man in his early 40s had a long history of being terrified that he was going to die suddenly of a heart attack at any time. Then he did have a heart attack, although he didn't die from it. Seeing that he was going to live after all, his fear of dying disappeared, although only temporarily. After a couple of months his terrible fear of dying returned. I never got a chance to analyze this man's anxiety.

Once a patient brought his wife into one of the sessions. She told me that she used to stutter. Then one day, she let her father have it verbally in no uncertain terms. She never stuttered again after that! The repressed anger Freud spoke about was **expressed** and was no longer repressed, so the symptom left.

Finally, I was treating a lady who had very severe depression. One day, her brother came to the session with her. He told me that he had suffered from extreme anxiety for a number of years. He had tried all sorts of combinations of medicines without any success. Then one day, he said to himself, "the hell with it" and threw away all his medicines. His anxiety disappeared that day never to return.

I made a point of telling all my patients with anxiety this last story. That patient had finally let go of his repressed anger. It's not easy to let go of anger, as almost everyone knows. Sometimes it seems like the therapist has to listen to the anger over and over again for a long time, until the patient comes to the realization that holding onto it is ruining his/her life. However, it is usually useless to try to point this fact out to them in order to speed up the process.

I used to think it isn't fair that people who explode in anger are able to let go of it after exploding, while the person subjected to the anger, then carries it around for long periods. If the person who is subjected to the anger fights back, often the fight goes back and forth ad infinitum. If this weren't true, many therapists would have no work to do.

▧ Sociopathy ▰▰▰▰▰▰▰▰▰▰▰▰▰▰▰▰▰▰▰▰

As part of our training, we went to talk to prison inmates. First, we were told that if we were taken hostage, we shouldn't expect anyone to come to our rescue. We were also told to tell any of the inmates assigned to us that, if they were threatening harm to anyone, we could not keep it confidential. Furthermore, if they spoke of any murders in the past, they would have to disguise the facts such that we would be unable to testify in court about it. The first inmate I saw got up and left, never to come back, after I told him he would have to disguise any facts about any murders.

Part of the time, I was assigned to facilitate a group of drug addicts. One of the group members said, "What we need is discipline". Upon thinking this over, I decided that discipline, if administered fairly, is a part of caring.

During a session with the group, one of the group members asked me if I knew how George Washington died. I repeated the story I had heard about his riding out in the cold and then developing pneumonia, of which he subsequently died. The inmate then told me that this was not the real truth. He said, actually, Martha had come home unexpectedly one day while George Washington was upstairs in the bedroom with one of the maids. So, he then jumped out the window, fractured his arm, which became infected, and this was what caused his death. The inmate added, "If you don't believe me, read 'Ford's True Biography of George Washington'. Later, when I had the time, I went to the Harvard library of rare books and read in Ford's True Biography that George Washington had indeed gone out riding in the cold, when he caught pneumonia, and had died as a result of that. Cheaters and liars are cynics and always prefer to believe that everyone is dishonest.

Speaking with antisocial personalities convinced me that, by and large, they did not receive the love and caring to which all children are entitled. I believe that, generally, it is the love for the parent which enables people to control their impulses., in other words they have incorporated a loving superego or conscience. Attempts to provide that love after children have reached adolescence is rarely successful in rehabilitating them.

In the clinic, one ex-convict told me that he purposely got into fights when out of prison, so that he would be put back into prison. He told me he hated all people and, even while in prison, he would cause trouble so the guards would put him in solitary confinement, which, he said, was the only place where he felt comfortable.

Another young man I saw was addicted to opiates. He was an only child, his father wasn't around, and his mother neglected him. I don't recall the details, but what he told me made it clear that his mother was never there for him. One time, he told me about how he would stick a needle in his ear to cause bleeding, after which he would run into an emergency room screaming, pretending to be in pain. I asked him what the opiates did for him. He described vividly how warm and comfortable he felt when he took them. I could easily imagine a little baby, cradled in its mother's arms, feeling just the same way this young man did when he took the opiates. This is what had been missing in his life and this is what he felt he needed.

A young man whom I saw during my training told me about an incident where he picked up two young women and, at gunpoint, forced them to get into his truck. He drove them a short distance, then let them go unharmed. He spoke of how, when he was small, while his father was in the garage fixing a car, he would go out to the garage to look. His father would tell him to get out, saying angrily, "You're nothing but a puppy dog!" I could imagine his feeling crestfallen and rejected. This must have been representative of his father's usual treatment of him, consequently he grew up feeling small and worthless. Criminals often describe how forcing someone to obey them at gunpoint makes them feel big and powerful, thus relieving their feeling small and worthless.

A divorced woman came in because she was addicted to tranquilizers. One of her sons came to the office with her. He had been in jail, and since he had gotten out, he had started his own business and he made it a point to hire ex-convicts to work for him. He said he knew how they felt. It turned out that, as a young boy, his father had told him, "You're no good, you've been no good since the day you were born, and you'll never be any good". He had been put in jail for abusing drugs. He learned how his fellow inmates felt so he wanted to help them feel worthwhile.

From where I sit, the cause of the opioid crisis and the development of sociopathic personalities often seems readily apparent. Also, it seems that our society is doing a very poor job of preventing these problems and as a result, innocent people in our society have to pay the price, in the form of drug addiction, murder, and crime.

■ Transference

A married woman in her 40s came to see me because of anxiety and depression. She complained of feeling anxiety when she was at the grocery store, waiting to pay. At such times, she said her legs felt like jelly and wobbly on her feet. She was in an unhappy marriage and, as a child she had gotten little affection from her father. She missed receiving affection from the men in her life. I recall her telling me of a time when her husband intentionally dropped a stack of books right beside her while she was fast asleep, waking her with a shock. She turned to propositioning men for the attention she felt was missing. In one session she told me she had even propositioned the taxi driver who brought her to our appointment. One day sitting in her chair across from me in my office, she sat clasping her hands together, bending forward with her elbows in her lap, pleading, "Dr. Green, I want you!" I recognize now how critical such interactions are to whether treatment will prove helpful, but at the time, I didn't know what to say, so I said nothing. A kind, fatherly response, such as how loving fathers respond to their little daughters would have been therapeutic, such as, "I hope I can help you truly satisfy desires like that in your other relationships."

Sometime later a lady came to me when her psychiatrist had retired. She told me that this previous psychiatrist had had sex with her many times. She added that she loved him. Prior to her therapy with him, she hadn't felt worthy of being loved by a man, and she felt that the therapy with her psychiatrist had cured her of that belief. Later, when I was seeing that patient's sister, I was told that my former patient, her sister, had not been happy with my therapy. In addition, the former patient had, in the mean time, gotten married! The sexual relationship with her therapist had seemed to work out well; however, in too many cases trespassing this boundary turns out to be harmful. I prefer to believe that my not having sex with her led her to seek a loving relationship elsewhere, now that she felt worthy of being loved by a man.

Years later, I saw a married lady in her early 50s who had been admitted to the hospital after making a suicide attempt. Despite having a loving husband and two good children, she often felt she wanted to be left alone in her room. She said she had had depressions all her life and that she had contemplated suicide since she was a little girl. Growing up, she, her mother, and siblings were terrorized by a tyrannical and physically abusive father. She told of how she would be asleep at night when her father would come into her room, pull her out of the bed, and start beating her. One day, she confided in a teacher, showing her the bruises on her back. However, there was nothing that could be done because her father was a prominent citizen who was respected by everyone in the town. Attempting to explain her father's treatment of her, she said she was the only one who ever talked back to him. Although being uncertain of it at first, she finally realized that the abuse had actually occurred. While in college, she met the man whom she later married, but the depressions continued nevertheless.

After about three years in therapy, she related how she felt her intimate relations with her husband were lackluster. She told me that she thought she would be happy if she spent time with me, and hinted at wanting to be intimate with me, although, she felt guilty about these feelings. I said to her that such feelings are nice feelings and we wanted her to be able to experience such feelings, but we were not going to act on them. As the feelings of depression faded, they were replaced by good feelings about herself. Her desire for me also seemed to fade and her sexual relations with her husband began to feel more fulfilling. After therapy ended, she continued sending me postcards occasionally, writing, "I never believed I could be as happy as I am now".

How did I feel? I patted myself on the back for how well I handled this therapy. I felt that I finally had learned how to deal with transference love.

One of my earliest patients was a young single woman who used to spend the sessions sitting on the floor at my feet. During the course of the therapy she admitted herself to a psychiatric unit. Her psychiatrist there asked me to come in for a joint session together with my patient. There, he told me that she had told him she was in love with me, and in front of her, asked me what I had to say about that. Being put on the spot, all I could think of saying was, "Well, I'm not in love with her". I didn't think too kindly of that psychiatrist. However, on thinking about it, I felt if I were her and had confessed to someone that I was in love with them, I would find a clear rejection kinder than any sort of circumlocution. The patient did continue seeing me in my office after being discharged, so I imagine she wasn't too hurt. Unfortunately, I have no knowledge of how she did after we terminated.

Also, early in my practice, a lady I was seeing, one day came in saying she had to have one of her ovaries removed and she was terrified. As we both stood up at the end of that session, she put her arms around me as if she were going to kiss me. I put my hands up to keep a distance between us. While she was in the hospital, I went to visit her. Later when she came back to see me in my office, I asked her what she would have thought if we had kissed that previous time. She replied that she never would have been able to come back to see me again. However, I never asked her why, and so I missed a learning opportunity.

An attractive young lady sought therapy because she found herself angry at men for always concentrating so much of their attention on her breasts.

I didn't say much of anything as I understood her anger, that they merely showed interest in a part of her body rather than in her as a person. After a few months of therapy, she wanted to stop the sessions, but she asked me if she could continue to see me, but without having to pay. I told her that she would have to continue to pay. Stupid me didn't realize what she was saying. Now, with hindsight, I can see that she had developed transference feelings for me, which I should have explored together with her at that point. The simple rejection of her advance had obviated any work on the deeper issue.

Finally, I learned something when a woman patient spoke of how kind and caring one of the hospital doctors was, when she added, "But, boy is he ugly!" Later, another woman speaking about the same doctor said, "And he is the handsomest man!" Beauty is in the eye of the beholder, and so, I guess, are feelings of love.

◼ Alcohol ▬▬▬▬▬▬▬▬▬▬▬▬▬▬▬▬▬▬▬▬▬

Over the years I saw a number of alcoholics, and so I often was reminded of the saying, "Everyone talks about my drinking but no-one talks about my thirst".

One middle-aged lady was such a bad alcoholic that after many failed attempts at various forms of treatment, she was finally committed to a nursing home. Once there, even though she could have escaped at any time to go out to drink, she never did. Instead, she stopped drinking and was completely satisfied being confined with the demented women in the nursing home. Apparently, to be taken care of like a child was what she needed - not alcohol. Artzybasheff painted a picture of a naked person hugging a giant wine bottle with two breasts. Alcoholism is the thirst for the loving mother.

A young man I saw in the clinic had been in an auto accident. As a result, he now had a paralyzed left arm. He explained that he was driving drunk when it happened. I said, "That's too bad.", but to my surprise, he replied, "It's actually the best thing that could have happened to me!". I said, "How so?" He answered, "It made me realize that I had to stop partying. Otherwise, I probably would have continued partying the rest of my life."

Another young man told me that his wife divorced him because of his drinking. When I asked if he was still drinking, he told me that he had stopped drinking completely. I asked him why he wasn't drinking now. He replied, "I no longer need to" (now that he was no longer with his wife). That seemed to contradict the little ditty:

> He drinks he thinks because she nags.
> She nags, she thinks because he drinks.
> But neither will admit what's true,
> That he's a drunk, and she's a shrew.

A lady I saw told me that while drunk, her brother dove into a swimming pool, fractured his neck after which he was paralyzed from the neck down. When asked what he thought of drinking after that, he replied that it wasn't the fault of alcohol. He blamed what happened on the pool!

A fellow I had been seeing intermittently for many years explained that he came to see me whenever his wife couldn't stand his coming home drunk every evening. When this would occur, he would come back to see me again and would stop drinking. However, after a brief period of sobriety he would start drinking again. The cycle would occur repeatedly. When I asked him what alcohol did for him, he said, "When I'm sober, everything looks 'blah' and after having a drink, the world looks colorful and exciting again". You can have the best spouse in the world and still long for the loving mother you didn't have.

It surprised me that a number of people who appeared to be floridly psychotic when I first saw them, became normal as soon as they stopped drinking. Patients who were bipolar, namely those requiring hospitalization because of manic episodes, could not drink a single drink without it setting off a recurrence of mania. I routinely told those patients with bipolar disorder that alcohol was poison for them.

■ Murder

I saw only one person who committed murder. He was a young man who impulsively strangled his fiancé when she told him she was breaking up with him. As a result, he spent ten years in prison. I saw him shortly after he was released. He looked like a broken man. He was extremely polite, as if he were apologizing for being alive. I think no duration of time nor amount of treatment could ever have eased his guilt about what he had done. The message I took away from the brief time I saw him, was that women who are thinking of breaking off a relationship should do so in steps, breaking it to them gently. If afraid of doing it even gently, don't give any warning - just go far away, once you have decided.

This next case is an example of the warning: Listen to your gut. I was working in a clinic, writing prescriptions for patients in treatment with psychologists and social workers. While I was seeing her husband, his wife telephoned me frantically saying she was terrified that her husband might kill her. He had that scary flat affect. I sent a note to his therapist saying I believed the man was psychotic and he should have him committed, despite the fact that he had been discharged from the hospital recently. Later, the treating psychologist told me that he had had a joint meeting with the man and his wife. He said that he concluded that the man was not actively homicidal. Shortly thereafter, the man did murder his wife. I could not tolerate working with patients if I were not in control of the case. so I left that job.

You have to listen to your gut. Restraining orders don't seem to prevent murders by jilted lovers. Reporting to the police does not help as the police can't do anything until after the crime has been committed. Although it is difficult to do, moving far away, remaining incognito, seems like the only safe way. I, myself, would do either that or carry a pistol and if the guy broke the restraining order and came to see me anyway, I would shoot both of his kneecaps while backing off.

For some time I was prescribing for a young lady who had divorced her ex-marine husband. She never dared to date as she knew her ex would kill her and any man she dated. She described his character and I could understand why she felt the way she did. They had a young daughter and he was a good father to her, but he was absolutely controlling - never allowing any ifs ands or buts. He was a heroic soldier, and the army called him up for assignments when they needed him, but he was not to be trusted as a husband.

I also briefly saw a young husband who beat his 2 year old daughter whenever he was babysitting her while his wife was out. His wife quickly kicked him out and later divorced him. He couldn't really explain his anger at his baby daughter (the anger was deeply lodged in his unconscious). During the visits he speculated on a connection with a young girl cousin who had been favored over him when he was little, but he felt no emotional connection to it. Over the years I saw other examples of where old feelings of rage would pop up in inexplicable situations. People sometimes feel powerful impulses to do something, not aware of why. And they find themselves acting on these impulses in ways they later regret.

When the news carries stories of mass murderers and serial killers, people always ask, "You're a psychiatrist. Why do they do it?" From my reading about people like Ted Bundy, Jeffrey Dahmer, and David Berkowitz, I am convinced the answer lies in old memories buried deeply in the unconscious. When observing infants and the very young, one can see that when frustrated, they exhibit terrible rage, and if never defused by parental love, that rage can resurface later in life, the individual being totally unaware of its origin. Most murderers when asked why they did it, answer, "I don't know". Again we see a disorder of love and the lack of a caring superego.

Love

One married woman whom I had seen every three months for years for medication prescribing, never told me very much about herself until she was in her late 70s, when she was diagnosed with colon cancer. She usually came to appointments with her husband. They appeared to have a normal relationship. However, she eventually told me that she had a longstanding love affair with her priest, although it was clear that this was a delusion. It had never been mentioned during her previous visits.

After she died, her husband came in and told me that, from the beginning of their marriage, she had never permitted him to have sexual intercourse with her. Upon relating this to me, he said, "I told her I couldn't live like that - but I guess I did."

For some years I treated a married man who carried around a little black book with all the names and telephone numbers of women he could call at any time for sex. He eventually took one of these women across the state line, against her will. She filed kidnapping charges against him, so he was sent to the state hospital for the criminally insane. He called me again when he was released, saying to me, "I made the mistake of falling in love with her." After some time, his wife came in to see me. She was an attractive woman. She knew all about her husband's philandering, but she accepted it and didn't want any other man but him.

Another married man in his 30s came to see me because he had a compulsion to drive downtown after work to pick up men for homosexual trysts. Later his wife came in once by herself. She also knew all about her husband's behavior and told me that she had loved nobody but him, since they first met each other in high school. (This was in the days before AIDS) The therapy with him was brief and, I believe, effected very little.

Which reminds me of an obviously gay man who became depressed after his partner of many years died. They had been happy together for twenty years. He proudly showed me a photo of a handsome young man. During the sessions, he spoke of the many liaisons he had been having since his partner's death. His manner was always light hearted and jovial. Despite its sometimes being difficult listening to his graphic depictions of his sexual exploits, I couldn't help but like him. He seemed to get a kick out of all the married men he hooked up with. He enjoyed the idea that he was more exciting to them than their wives. (He knew I was married, so it was clear what message he was sending to me.) He even made more explicit sexual overtures to me, which I simply let pass. One time I bumped into him in the hallway and, as I had warm feelings towards him, I recall having the impulse to put my arm over his shoulder, as if he were a buddy. However, as I knew he would take it the wrong way, I desisted. But the impulse had been there. Eventually he came down with cancer of the liver and died. I missed him. His attitude that life was fun and games was infectious and entertaining.

A young married man in his 30s came to me because for some time, besides his wife, he had been carrying on with two single women. He said he wanted to stop this behavior, but he felt compelled to continue. His two paramours knew about each other, and each was angry about the other. It wasn't clear whether his wife knew about them or whether she just chose to ignore it. But most interesting to me was his childhood history. His family lived in the middle floor of a three story house. One aunt lived in the apartment above, and the other aunt lived in the apartment below. As a child, he rotated between sleeping with his mother and alternating sleeping with either of his two aunts. He was repeating this pattern with his wife and the two mistresses. There we see Freud's Repetition Compulsion again. He didn't remain in therapy very long, probably because his motivation to change was not very strong.

Another married man moved out of his home when he turned 40, leaving behind a wife and two children. He still loved them and continued to return to do chores and repairs and to provide for his wife and children, but he felt the need to have his own place. He explained that his father had died when he was young, so as the oldest, he had to act as the man of the house. Now, he just wanted to have a place of his own for the first time in his life. His wife needed some counseling to help her adjust to the change. Sometimes people react to the compulsion to repeat old patterns by striving to do the opposite.

Once, in the middle of weekly therapy sessions, a married woman notified me that she would not be coming in the following week. She explained that she was meeting a man, not her husband, at that time for a tryst. I told her that I would not bill her insurance for that hour and she would have to pay me out of pocket. I felt she was using our scheduled time both to cover herself and as a way of asking for my approval of what she was doing. I didn't want to approve nor disapprove. People have to live with the consequences of their actions, whether they were discovered or not. Interestingly, when I told her she would have to pay for that time, she changed her mind and came in for that appointment after all. Her decision to have an affair was something which should be discussed prior to acting it out and and needing to talk about the fallout afterwards.

The next two patients prompted me to ask myself, "What is love, anyway?"

I saw one man's wife as a patient when she was already in her 60s. I heard from a relative of hers that when she was young, she would turn all men's eyes, as she was so beautiful. Furthermore, she would bestow her favors on all the men around, including her husband's best friends. Her husband never seemed to notice; he idolized her, no matter what. By the time I started seeing her, she had mostly lost her looks, but she retained her flirtatious manner. After some time, she died of one of her chronic medical conditions. Her husband continued to be devoted to her and the memory of her. This is truly an example of undying adoration.

The other patient was an exceptionally beautiful young Hispanic girl who had stabbed her boyfriend with a knife in a jealous rage. She had caught him cheating on her, which was nothing new. (No-one he would have cheated on her with could have been more beautiful than she) She seemed to agree that she needed to break up with this boyfriend as next time she might kill him, but when I saw her again, she told me they were back together. When I asked her why she took him back, she replied, "Isn't that what love is?" For some people, I guess so.

So what do I think is the answer to the question of what love is. I don't know - I'm just a psychiatrist.

Suicide

I was asked to see a man in the hospital who was saying he wanted to die. He had been a cement mason who one day had to work alone, as his partner was unable to be there to assist him. He was a very powerful, muscular man who thought he could lift the heavy machinery off the back of his truck by himself. When he did, he heard pop-pop-pop in his lower back. At first he thought nothing of it, however, the next day, he started to experience lower back pain, which since then continued day after day unabated. He went to an orthopedic surgeon who told him that there was nothing he could do for him. A number of other surgeons also told him they would not operate, until he finally found one orthopedic surgeon who agreed to do the surgery. Postoperatively, he found that he was wheelchair-bound due to weakness of both legs. Furthermore, he was incontinent of both urine and feces. He felt like he was a broken man and wanted to commit suicide. I never learned what happened to him.

I saw another young man who was working with a concrete mixer when part of his clothing got caught in the mixer and he was pulled into it. One of his coworkers saw what was happening and turned off the switch. His life was saved, but in the process, he had sustained fractures of his neck accompanied by constant unremitting neck pain. The surgeons told him there was nothing they could do for him and that the pain was probably not going to get better. The pain was so bad he couldn't sleep, he couldn't read, he couldn't think, he couldn't watch TV, etc. He couldn't do anything. He felt the pain had rendered him completely useless. He couldn't relate to his wife or children because of the pain, and after a few months, he got a divorce. I prescribed something, but it didn't give much relief. It wasn't much later when I heard that he killed himself. After having witnessed his suffering for a few months, I could well understand his decision. One would have to be there to listen to him, visit after visit, to really witness his degree of suffering.

I was asked to do a competency evaluation on an elderly lady who was refusing to undergo an amputation of her gangrenous foot. The surgeon told her she would die if the foot were not removed, but she steadfastly refused any surgery. The surgeon wanted to know from me whether she was legally competent to refuse. I asked her the three questions which comprise my evaluation of competency: 1) Do you understand what the issue is? She replied that the surgeon wanted to amputate her foot, and she was refusing to have it done; 2) Do you understand what will happen if you don't have it done? She answered that she knew that would lead to her death; and 3) What would you do if the surgeon indicated that he would do the amputation against your will? She replied that she would call a lawyer. As a result, I declared her legally competent to refuse the surgery. I later heard that this particular case was written up in the law books. A few weeks later, I heard from the surgeon that the foot began to hurt so bad that she decided to agree to the amputation.

Before my mother developed Alzheimer's, she asked me whether I would help her end her life, if she were to lose her mental abilities. I told her that I would not help her and that she would have to make that decision on her own. By the time she did develop Alzheimer's at age 86, she no longer had the ability to carry out her wish, despite the fact that she had accumulated a large cache of pills. Her dementia gradually worsened over a nine year period. Even prior to the onset of her dementia, she had made it clear to her doctor that she wanted no extraordinary medical means to extend her life. She finally died a peaceful death from untreated kidney failure. I often think about what I would do in my mother's situation. The truth is that I don't know.

At this point in my writing, you might think that I don't know much about anything. You'd be right.

■ Prescribing

During my 46 years in practice, I wrote many prescriptions; however, my main interest was in talking to patients and getting to know them. And so, I will just mention two dramatic examples of patients who responded very well to medication.

When Prozac first came out, I was referred a married lady in her 40s who had a germ phobia such that she had to wash her hands after touching anything. She had been in therapy with a psychologist friend of mine for many years, however, the symptom stubbornly persisted. After taking a shower and turning the faucet off, she had to wash her hands again. She avoided petting the family dog. Her symptom apparently effected her self-esteem as she dressed and made herself up like an uptight school marm, like the portrait of Emily Dickinson. Although I had not yet prescribed Prozac, I had read about its use in

Canada, so I decided to prescribe it for her. It worked like a miracle. She was able to give up her compulsive hand washing and she blossomed in her outward appearance as a result. Her countenance became cheery and smiling, and she let her hair hang down, its waving back and forth as she turned her head, instead of being tied tightly back. As a result, her husband was afraid she was having an affair, and his behavior with her changed to obsequiousness and fawning. Everyone at her work remarked about the change in her. Incidentally, she was not the type to cheat on her husband.

The other patient I will mention was also in her early 40s and had been in therapy for many years. Her complaint was that she would break down crying unpredictably for no reason she could fathom. She told me she would stop her car at a red light and suddenly break down crying. Although she had also been in therapy for a long time, her symptom also stubbornly persisted. Again, the Prozac worked like a miracle, almost immediately after starting it, and eliminated the symptom.

I never got to learn the psychodynamics of these patients as they were in therapy with other practitioners. But for me, the quick and easy amelioration of symptoms did not make up for the absence of learning how personalities develop. I still wanted to learn what made people tick.

Mistakes

While still in training, I once sought advice from one of my supervisors as to how to respond to a patient. I said I was afraid of saying the wrong thing. He said to me, "If your heart is in the right place, there's not too much you can say wrong." This helped me in many situations which arose. However, on looking back, I realize that I did still make many mistakes.

One young lady came to me saying she wanted to get rid of her boyfriend whose name was "Jim". During the second session, she made a slip of the tongue and instead of saying, "I want to dump Jim", she said, "I want to jump Jim." When I pointed out the slip to her, she turned bright red and the next visit she told me she wanted to quit the therapy. Looking back on it, I should not have pointed out the slip to her as it was the side of her conflict which she stated she wanted to rid herself of. If it happened later on in the treatment I could have said something like, "It seems like the physical aspect of the relationship is hard for you to give up." Some time later, a colleague told me of a male patient of his that made the following slip, in which he said, "Why is it I always feel guilty after having sex with my mother?" My colleague was wise enough to remain silent. Most men would rather not be aware of such incestuous wishes.

The next mistake was one I wanted to whip myself for after it occurred. I was seeing a couple. The man told me he came home unexpectedly one day from work to find his wife in bed. When he opened the bedroom closet door to hang up his jacket, there was his best friend standing completely naked. Immediately upon hearing that, I broke out laughing. All I could think was, "Just like in the movies!" The man in this couple did say, "I guess it is kind of funny", but that didn't assuage my guilt. I later heard the couple got a divorce. Small wonder. At least he didn't shoot his wife and his best friend, although in some countries this would be pardonable. Two lessons to be learned from this incident are: 1) don't own a gun or you might do something you will regret; and 2) if you are going to come home early from work, telephone your wife first. If she is the cheating kind, it will likely come out eventually at a less inauspicious time.

A young man came to me because he was having a problem with his anger at his wife. Whereas he had saved himself for when he got married, his wife had not. She apparently had had many sexual relationships before she met him. He found it very difficult to accept this and was taking his anger out on his wife. He didn't know how he wanted to deal with it. At one point I said to him that maybe she was sexually active to satisfy her curiosity about men. I think this was a strategic error, and subsequently he did not show up for the next appointment. In retrospect I realized that he didn't want me to make an excuse for his wife, but rather he wanted to focus on his feelings about a simple reality. By excusing his wife, I obviously didn't seem to understand how he was feeling. I should have been more like Carl Rogers and said, "I see that you are in terrible pain because your wife's attitude towards sexual relations is not the same as yours".

In conclusion, I probably made many mistakes most of which I never became aware of. I always tried to see to it that my heart stayed in the right place. One lady for whom I was prescribing medications, came down with a serious disease. I remarked, "xyzosis is a difficult disease to treat." My comment was totally unnecessary and merely added to her worries at that moment. She soon decided to obtain her psychiatric medications elsewhere.

Homesickness

A Japanese woman was referred to me because she was depressed. She had married an American soldier after World War II and had moved to the U.S. with him. When I saw her they had an 18 year old son. During the sessions, she spoke of how much she missed her mother and how she wished she were in Japan again. However, it was clear that her husband and son would not go with her if she decided to leave. After I stopped seeing her, I heard that she had moved back to Japan.

I saw a young Taiwanese man who had come here to study engineering. When he completed his studies, he sent for his girlfriend and they got married here. However, shortly after they had married, his young wife decided to return to Taiwan, even though he remained here.

When I was 27, I married a nurse who was from Sweden. Although we got along reasonably well, she was never very happy in the U.S. She never gave up her Swedish citizenship and it was a standing joke in the family that, according to her, everything - the flowers, the medical care, the lakes, the treatment of the elderly and disabled, etc.- was better in Sweden. When our youngest was born, my wife began to complain incessantly of back pain. She went to numerous doctors about it and even underwent surgery, all of which was only of minimal help. She was convinced that the doctors in Sweden were better at treating back pain. An Orthopedic surgeon, whom I respected, had seen her and told me he felt the problem was psychological.

When I attended one of her psychotherapy sessions with her, I noticed that first she spoke about her back pain. But then, suddenly, she began talking about Sweden. Her therapist said, "You wish you were back in Sweden". After the session, it struck me that she associated 'back' pain and her desire to be 'back' in Sweden. When I told her I thought her pain was psychological, she said, "You think everything is psychological!" Not long after, we divorced, and she moved back to Sweden. There she contacted her old high school boyfriend and, subsequently, they moved in together. My older daughter, when she finished college, moved to the same town in Sweden so when I visited there five years later, my ex-wife's back was better, and she seemed to be in her element. She said that she felt she was as happy as she could be. I realize that I cannot prove that pain in her back was psychological, although I choose to believe that it was. And maybe the doctors in Sweden are actually better at treating back problems, but I doubt it.

Children

Not surprising, but interesting to me, was to see how parents effected the course of their children's lives.

I saw a married lady in her 70s who felt like the saddest, most bereft person in the world. She felt this bad about herself despite the fact that she had a loving husband who was devoted to her. Although she must have been very attractive when she was in college, she didn't have lots of boyfriends like her roommate did. She didn't even seem to have been envious of her fun-loving roommate. Her constant woe-is-me attitude must have turned the young men off. But she did find a husband. From his being someone who worked in the rehabilitation field, I would guess that he had a desire to rescue her. A history of her childhood seemed to point to where her low self-esteem stemmed from.

One incident, which she related, was indicative of the genesis of her problem. She was about 4 years old when one day she was waiting for her father to come home from work. As he stepped in the door, she ran up to him and jumped into his arms. Immediately, he pushed her forcefully away into the stairway across the vestibule. Her husband's devotion was unable to make up for her feelings of rejection. She had been in therapy for years before she was transferred to me. At 73, she had a stroke, which left her paralyzed on one side. I visited her a few times in the nursing home. It was painful to watch how much difficulty she had maneuvering her way around. After a short time, she died. Her husband was devastated and could no longer carry on the part-time job he had enjoyed before.

A pattern I saw frequently was of children's avoiding marriage ostensibly because they didn't want one like their parents'. For years I saw a lady whose husband treated her terribly. However, she was one of those delightful, cheery ladies whose smile would make your troubles seem to vanish in thin air. In fact, she was so loved in the company where she used to work that they promised her they would hire her again if ever she wished to return. Furthermore, she was very bright and had graduated near the top in college. She had helped her husband with his college courses. Nevertheless, he treated her as if she were stupid. At any rate, it was a bad marriage, and, by the time she came to see me, whenever separation was mentioned, she said she should have done that when she was still young enough, even though it was against her religion. But the effect her marriage had on the children was that none of them ever married nor had significant others by the time they were in their 40s. "If that's what marriage is like, I don't want it," might have been their motto. As I said, I saw many examples of this pattern.

A wealthy man came to see me, after he had already had a heart attack, because he wanted to improve his relationships with his wife and children.

He told me that when he was growing up he always saw his parents fighting over money. He told himself that money was the problem, so he decided he was going to accumulate loads of it. He told me he didn't care whom he stepped on in order to get the money. The result was that he was very rich, but also very nasty. At home he ruled the roost and was aware that his wife and children disliked him. He wanted to change that and become a better husband and father. However, he frequently canceled appointments saying he had to travel to Timbuktu for an important business meeting. We didn't have many sessions before he had another heart attack and died. From my point of view, he learned the wrong lesson from watching his parents' marriage. As parents, we don't really know what lessons our children take from experiencing their childhoods with us.

One time I was talking with one of my male patients about winning the lottery. He had lived in a number of foster homes when he was growing up. One foster mother disciplined him by grabbing both of his feet and dunking him headfirst into a tub of water. When she thought it had been long enough, she lifted him out, with him choking and gasping. Eventually he was sent to live with a family of gypsies. He said they treated him with love and he loved them. He told me he sent them cards and visited them periodically over the years. So I asked him what he would do with the money if he won the lottery. He answered that he would buy that gypsy family a beautiful second hand car. When I reflected upon this, I could see that he believed they valued second-hand things, as he, himself, was a second-hand boy.

Love is something, if you give it away, you end up getting more (as the song goes)

■ Miscellaneous ██████████████████████████████

The wife of a painfully shy man pushed him to get help. Among many other things, he was afraid to ask for a raise at work. Interestingly, when he first asked his wife for a date he said, "You wouldn't want to go out with me, would you?" He was consistent. In every way, he was afraid to assert himself. I agreed to see him for once weekly therapy. As is to be expected, he volunteered very little information about his emotions and about his childhood. So analyzing his character was not an option. I decided to use directive therapy, which consisted of my telling him to take his wife out to dinner at a nice restaurant once a week, to buy her flowers on Valentine's Day, to celebrate anniversaries by giving her special gifts, to telling her how nice she looks, etc. After a few months, he decided he wanted to discontinue our sessions, saying he thought he should see a hypnotist instead. My thinking was that by giving, especially to those you love, you find that you feel better about yourself -that by being "generous'", you generate or are productive. Even our "genes" generate us. And when you are productive, you feel you are accomplishing something. After he stopped treatment, I never saw him again. However, I later heard from the physician who had referred him to me, that his wife had said that he had improved and that she attributed this to my therapy with him.

I saw a young mother in the clinic because she felt guilty about her daughter's being born with a heart defect. During our sessions, she mentioned that she was the type of person who, if the other person in the room fell down and just then a third person walked in, she would automatically say, "I didn't do it !" Otherwise, she was mostly silent during the sessions, although she would sit across from me constantly buffing the little brass knob on her pocketbook. I felt as if she were hypnotizing me. When the therapy came to an end, I realized that we had never discussed sex at all, so I asked her whether she had any problems in that area. She replied that when she first came in for treatment, she was having problems that way, but they gradually disappeared as the sessions progressed. I subsequently asked myself whether the constant shining of that little brass knob was symbolic of something sexual. I will leave that to the reader's imagination.

An 80 year old nurse was someone I will never forget. She was chronically deeply depressed. She was never married, had no close relatives, and no friends. She did have one relative who stopped by occasionally, although apparently they were not especially close. She had worked all of her life in one of the famous Boston hospitals, so I assumed she was good at her work. From where she lived and from how she spoke, I surmised that she came from a well-to-do old New England family. What particularly struck me was the way she spoke. Like they said about Dylan Thomas, no matter what she was talking about, it was like beautiful poetry emanating from her mouth. I wished I could have recorded everything she said. One time I asked her how she had traveled to my office. She replied, "By shank's mare" - an expression I had never heard before. Hearing that was like getting a glimpse of the time before automobiles. I was disappointed when on the second visit, she decided she didn't want to continue therapy. As the months went by, I thought repeatedly about her and what a pleasure it was just listening to her speak. I finally got up the nerve to call her to ask if I could drop by, just as a friend, explaining how much I enjoyed listening to her. She refused to allow it. I thought what a pity it was that this lady's words were lost to humanity. I had no idea whether I could help her with her depression, but that was not the reason I called her.

A young lady who had made a serious suicide attempt used to sit motionless in her chair across from me, not saying anything. In an attempt to prompt some dialogue, I resorted to commenting upon how she sat, the clothes she wore, her jewelry or whatever I could think of. The earrings she wore were miniature gold nooses. Finally, I said that by my attempting to analyze everything, I felt I was talking more about myself than about her. To this she remarked, "Go right ahead. It might do you some good". The therapy did help her, although I feel it was other parts of the hospital treatment which made the difference.

One day in the doctors' dining room, I heard a couple of the doctors talking about a man with terminal cancer who had developed an inguinal hernia. Together they decided that despite the fact that the man was going to die soon, they would do a surgical repair anyway. They realized that if they told him they wouldn't do the surgery, they would be saying to him that it was no use because he would be dead soon anyway. They felt it would be kinder to allow him to continue to have hope. The surgery wasn't medically necessary, but they cared about his feelings and so labeled the operation "psychosurgery". As I see it, they cared about the whole patient. The medical insurance companies would not have understood, but shouldn't caring take priority?

$\mathcal{L}$ONG TERM CASES

Miss Walsh came to see me when she was about 18 years old. She wanted help getting over her shyness. The therapy continued for about 5 years. Just before she first came in, she had been preparing to become a nun, when she suddenly decided to leave the novitiate and seek help with her shyness. She was very quiet spoken, so that I had to strain my ears to hear what she was saying. There were long periods of silence. She dressed drably, mostly in shades of gray. In the beginning, she reminded me of Eleanor Roosevelt. I listened very carefully, waiting for her to say something. When she did say something, it seemed to be fraught with meaning. It was like waiting patiently for nuggets of gold. Maybe I valued her utterances so much because I, myself, had been painfully shy when young, and felt, by listening to her, I might learn more about myself.

She told me she was the youngest of 5 and the only girl. She said that her brothers always ridiculed her. At one point she brought me in a list of Don'ts for rearing children. Among other things, it said, if you ridicule your children, they will grow up to be shy. On speaking about her tendency to be overly cautious, she compared it to carrying a very valuable plate across the room, being so afraid you might drop it, that you wanted to drop it on purpose, just to relieve the fear and tension,

On talking about going to singles' dances, she told me that she always refused a young man who asked the first time, but if he returned and asked her again, then she would agree to dance. I remember identifying with those young men, but feeling I wouldn't dare to come back and ask again. She was selecting young men who weren't shy like she was.

As time passed, it was amazing to see the change in her. In very slow increments, she changed to wearing colorful clothing, and she began to speak with more varied intonation, thus exhibiting more emotion. She told me of her interest in philosophy and of reading Kierkegaard, Simone Weil, Sartre, etc. Towards the end of our time together, she said that one of the nuns had once said to her that she shouldn't expect to enjoy herself here on earth, but that her reward would be in heaven, after she died. She strongly objected to this, saying, "I don't want to wait until I die! I want to enjoy myself while I am alive!" She had become a changed young lady; she had blossomed into someone who was full of life.

After ending therapy she sent me occasional letters telling me how she was studying for a doctorate in philosophy. And she had gotten into a relationship with a young man who had pursued her relentlessly. Later, she wrote that she had gotten married. As she wanted me to meet her husband, we arranged a meeting. At that point in particular, I felt like I was her father. I learned that simply listening non-judgmentally, permitted some people to let the person buried inside them come out into the open. This has been referred to as 'Self Actualization'. I believe there are many people out there who would like to accomplish the same thing.

#2

Miss Brown was single and in her 30s when she first came to see me. She said she didn't want to live but was not intending to try suicide.

She was not out of touch with reality. You would not even suspect that she was depressed unless she told you. Despite her depression, she frequently made funny cynical comments. She liked to entertain people with her sense of humor. She would speak of having a "gasoline ass", when talking about going by car. For example, when leaving she might say, "Be careful. But if you can't be careful, name it after me." I saw her over a period of many years, and this characteristic remained with her, no matter how bad the circumstances.

She had worked as a store detective, a job in which she had taken great pride. She described how she would pretend to drop her contact lens in front of the women's dressing room so she could look under the door to see if the woman she suspected was putting on a dress over her own clothing, planning on walking out of the store without paying. She said that she never lost a case when her arrests would go to court.

She had become depressed when one day, as she was apprehending a shoplifter, he picked up a shovel from a display and hit her on the head with it. She left work and was never able to return to work after that. It was as if that incident precipitated her loss of interest in life.

Miss Brown had been born in one of the famous old house-of-horrors for the insane to a mother whom she grew up to hate. She didn't know who her father was. As a young girl, she had been molested by her grandfather. When she was a teenager, her mother would march her to the family physician to see if she was still a virgin, -not an uncommon story. I don't know what else her mother did which caused her hatred, but when young, she used to stay out of the house as much as she could to avoid her mother. She entered competitive sports. She also spent a great deal of time on the streets. As soon as she could, she went to work, so she could earn enough money to move out of the house. She even changed her last name so that her mother could not find her. She generalized her hatred for her mother by carrying a dislike for all old women. But she was pleasant, sociable and friendly with her peers.

Although she grew up in a crime infested area, she did not have a coarse demeanor, nor did she speak like a ruffian.

She was never interested in men or sex. However, before I began seeing her, she had gone to a New Year's Eve party, and there she had sex for the one and only time in her life. As a result, she became pregnant. She carried the child to term, but, beforehand, arranged for its adoption. She told me that she didn't want a child because she knew she was incapable of being a good mother. When she was ready to deliver, she told the nursing staff that she definitely didn't want to see the baby at all. As fate would have it, the nurses brought the baby in to her room, whereupon, she instantly fell in love with her, and then, changed her mind about having her adopted and wanted to keep her. She decided to fight the adoption, but it was too late and she lost. The child was adopted by a well-to-do family in one of the suburbs. It wasn't long after that the incident where she was hit on her head at work and she felt she wished to die.

I met with her regularly over many years. She was never able to take on gainful employment again, despite being placed in a number of rehabilitation programs. She came down with diabetes, but she didn't take care of herself, as she didn't care about living. She often talked about not having a family and told me that I was her only family. Due to her not taking care of her diabetes, she developed heart disease. She ended up having heart surgery, almost dying of a postoperative infection.

When her daughter reached the age of 20, she made the effort to contact my patient, and they finally agreed to meet. Despite her having been brought up by a refined well-educated family, the daughter was a loose, foul-mouthed young woman who was the single mother to three children by three different men. Miss Brown took an immediate dislike to her daughter and never wanted to see her again after that first time.

Eventually her diabetes, left untended, wreaked further havoc and led to her having both legs amputated. Therefore, she was placed in a nursing home. I visited her there; she was in a wheelchair. I had never seen her crying before that time. Although she was never not depressed, she never showed any feelings of self pity. One day, when it seemed like she was not going to live much longer, I asked her what she thought it would be like after she died. True to her cynical personality she replied, "I don't give a shit !"

I went to her funeral. There, I saw her daughter with her three little children who were crawling all over their mother. She appeared to be a loving and affectionate mother, despite her uncouth demeanor. To me, this meant that although she had been brought up since birth in a good family, her uncouth mentality was determined by her genes, whereas her ability to love was determined by a combination of her genes and environment. Although Miss Brown had grown up in bad circumstances, she was always unselfish and considerate of people around her. I loved her and miss her. If there is a heaven, I hope to see her there.

#3

Over the years I saw many chronically psychotic patients. Some of them required regular visits over a long period of time. The lady I have described below came to my office every other week for a 50-minute session for about 30 years until I retired.

She first came to my attention with a complaint of constant buzzing in her head. The first thing I noticed about Miss Johnson was that she spoke like a little 5 year old girl. During the sessions, she talked mostly about her delusions. A number of times, she spoke of someone being inside her eating all her food, so that she had to eat a meal a second time as it wasn't she who had eaten the meal the first time. She had a vague sense of the unreality of her delusions, although they dominated her consciousness.

She worked as a filing clerk for a large company for a number of years. Once they began to computerize their records, she was unable to keep up with the changes and had to leave. She tried a number of menial jobs after that, but never lasted very long at any of them because she frequently stayed out due to her psychiatric symptoms, namely the voices and the bodily delusions. She once spoke to her mother about her delusions. Her mother cried upon hearing about it, realizing how much her daughter suffered. She was aware that she could not talk about them with anyone other than a psychotherapist or psychiatrist as she felt others wouldn't understand.

She lived by herself in supported housing. She didn't watch TV or go to the movies. She occasionally listened to Golden Oldies on the radio, but that was all. She had no friends and lived a very lonely existence, other than the fact that she visited her mother and siblings frequently. Her main enjoyment was going clothes shopping at Good Will stores.

Her father was "different". He made critical comments of everyone in the family. When Miss Johnson would begin a job, he would say to her: "You'll never last at it". He also put her brother down. The only way he contributed to the family was by stealing food from the grocery store and bringing it home. He frequently spent weeks away while staying with other women than his wife. Miss Johnson's mother often spoke of divorce, but never carried through with it. Strangely, when the father was with his family, he insisted on eating his meals off by himself. With me, he presented with a friendly demeanor. Occasionally he came to my office to pick up Miss Johnson. He smiled revealing terribly decayed teeth. He was a gambler but not a drinker. I imagined him being like a hillbilly from the Ozarks, without the moonshine, that is.

Although Miss Johnson was very attractive when she was young, she never was in a relationship. The few men who approached her quickly backed off. I imagine that if a young man were to make a pass at her, she would have no reaction at all, as if she were a statue without any feeling. Nevertheless, she had a delusion about one of the boys in her high school class. She believed that he occasionally visited her in her bed at night. She sometimes asked simple questions about the opposite sex like those a 5 year old girl might do, although she had no curiosity about where babies came from. During the many years over which I saw her, she never changed in that respect. In fact, there was very little change at all. She showed almost no feelings of joy, anger, or sadness. However, she never missed or was late for an appointment, and at the end of each session, she would always walk out saying, "Thank you, doctor."

Miss Johnson once asked me what her diagnosis was, to which I answered, Paranoid Schizophrenia. She simply accepted this without asking any further questions. Frequently she asked me whether I believed that she deserved to be collecting disability, as if she felt guilty about receiving the financial benefits. I always assured her that she was indeed disabled and deserved the money she received.

When I decided to retire, I was reluctant to tell her so, but when I did, she had no reaction, except to ask whom she was to see after I left. She never expressed any feelings about it. I felt bad about leaving her, although I don't really know what, if anything, she felt. I imagine if I asked her whether she was going to miss me, she would say, "Yes", but nothing more.

Once, before I started seeing Miss Johnson, a schizophrenic girl whom I had been treating for a while decided she wanted to discontinue therapy. During termination sessions, tears came to my eyes and I said I would miss her. She said nothing. Does flatness of affect mean absence of feeling or just absence of conscious feeling? It's hard to believe the feelings really aren't there somewhere.

■ #4 ▬▬▬▬▬▬▬▬▬▬▬▬▬▬▬▬▬▬▬▬▬▬▬▬▬▬

Mrs. Holmes was a married woman in her 40s who came in because of depression. She was unhappy in her marriage. They had a couple of children in their late teens who were doing well. The children were respectful and caring of both parents. Her husband was a decent provider and a good father. When asked why she wanted a divorce, the worst thing she could say about her husband was that he was boring. She had clearly been a good wife and mother over the past twenty years.

Her childhood had been horrific. Her father had had regular sexual intercourse with her since she was just 4 years old. Her mother witnessed this, but felt helpless to do anything about it. Furthermore, her father would tell my patient regularly how much he hated her. She told of one day when they were in a row boat when she fell overboard. She was struggling in the water, as she didn't know how to swim. Her father yelled at her saying he wished she would drown and die.

When she married, she decided she wanted to make a happy home like in the TV shows. And she did just that for about 20 years. In the beginning of therapy, she complained about her husband and how she didn't enjoy being with him. Then she spoke about how depressed she was. Finally she spoke of how her marriage had all been an act and that she could no longer keep pretending. Finally she divorced her husband.

After the divorce she began frequenting bars on the other side of the tracks, getting drunk, and befriending drunks and drug addicts. She was raped a couple of times, but didn't seem particularly upset about it. Her children stood by her through it all and tried to help her. While in this state she discontinued therapy.

Due to her childhood sexual and verbal abuse, understandably, Mrs. Holmes felt worthless. Once her children were old enough to be independent, she felt she couldn't pretend to be someone she felt she wasn't. The love from her children was unable to counterbalance this. Letting out what she felt was her true inner self relieved the tension of pretending. One of my own therapists had once told me that the job of a therapist is to help patients get to where they wanted to go, not where

I wanted them to go. I hope Mrs. Holmes will return to therapy some time in the future to work further on herself.

#5 ██

Mrs. Katz, a married lady in her 30s, was chronically depressed. She had a history of cutting her wrists and severing the tendons so that a hand surgeon had to repair them. She had been hospitalized many times, although she was not psychotic, that is, had no delusions, nor hallucinations, nor bizarre behavior. It was these signs which I considered the hallmarks of psychosis. In fact outwardly she appeared pleasant and jolly.

Mrs. Katz had grown up under very disordered circumstances. The family was very poor. She told of how they had to burn used sanitary napkins in the oven to keep warm in the winter. Her father was only around sporadically and unpredictably, when he would come home drunk. At those times, he terrorized the family with his frightening behavior. He eventually beat Mrs. Katz's mother so badly that she had to be confined to the state hospital for the remainder of her life due to the brain damage the father had inflicted upon her. As a result, when she was age 9, Mrs. Katz and her siblings were all sent to foster homes. Her foster father sexually molested her on a regular basis, although because he treated her kindly, she harbors no animosity towards him. In fact she told me she has warm feelings for him.

She ended up marrying a man who looked much like her terrible father - very tall with red hair. But in contrast to her father, he was a big teddy bear. She, herself, was like a roly-poly, naive 5 year old. She told me how very dependent she was on her husband, to the point that when he went to the bathroom to do his business, she had to be there with him. He went to work weekdays and provided for both of them. I recall her telling me that one day, while he was at work, she baked a cake for him, but before he came home, she ate the whole cake herself. She was very afraid that because she was getting so fat her husband would leave her.

I asked her to bring him in for a session so that we could talk about her fear. When she told her husband how afraid she was that he would leave her, he responded with, "I would never leave you!" and that he would love her no matter how fat she got to be. It was clear that the two of them were bonded by love despite her severe mental illness.

■ #6 ██

Mrs. Riley was in her early 30s when she was hospitalized because her bulimia. She had a bruise on the back of her hand from sticking her fingers down her throat to get herself to throw up. She told me that the only thing which helped her stop her bulimia was the drug, Valium. First I asked her about alcohol to which she answered that she drank very little, because, "More than one drink and I'm under the table." Her girlfriend, who was also in therapy with me, confirmed Mrs. W's story. So I prescribed the Valium for her, and, as with all patients, I made sure that she didn't use more than I prescribed.

Mrs. Riley spoke to me about her husband and about her family. Her husband sounded like a decent fellow. Her parents sounded like they were overly protective of her. As I recall, she hadn't been allowed to go out on a date before she was 21. I asked her to bring her husband in with her for one of our sessions, but she refused, saying, she was afraid he might make her look bad.

One day, after being in therapy for a couple of years, she came in looking exhausted and sick. She denied that she had been drinking and insisted that she was fine. Not long after, she called to tell me she was in the hospital with stomach pain. When I spoke to her husband, he told me that she had actually been drinking every night for some time. He said, when he got up in the middle of the night to go to the bathroom, he would trip over the empty bottles in the hallway.

I visited her in the Intensive Care Unit. There, in the hospital, she said the reason she hadn't told me about her drinking was because she thought

I would think badly of her. At the same time, she told me she was very afraid she might die the hospital. She asked me for a hug, which I gave her because I saw how terrified she was. A couple of days later, I was shocked to hear that she had died. Apparently, her stomach pain was due to pancreatitis caused by her drinking. In medical school, I had learned that drinking was a cause of pancreatitis and I had seen a number of such patients. I was aware that alcoholics often developed chronic abdominal pain for this reason. However, I was not aware that pancreatitis was so frequently fatal. Mrs. W was only 35 years old when she died.

I attended the wake. I felt very bad about her death. In the therapy, she had spoken of how very depressed she was, but she made it clear that she was not actively suicidal. She obviously valued our visits. We covered a lot of ground in our discussions, but she never let on that she was a closet drinker. Mrs. Riley wasn't the only patient who kept secrets from me. Keeping secrets from one's therapist often sabotages the effectiveness of the therapy. Furthermore, alcoholism can be a form of passive suicide. Because she drank at night on an empty stomach, she probably predisposed herself to pancreatitis. I recall hearing that alcohol on an empty stomach was particularly dangerous.

■ #7 ■■■■■■■■■■■■■■■■■■■■■■■■■■■■■■■■■■■■

When she came to see me, Miss Walker was a divorced women in her mid 40s with no children. She was depressed because her boyfriend, who was of her same age, had suddenly died of a heart attack. He was the love of her life. When he started having difficulty breathing, he tried to ignore it, because he didn't like going to doctors. (difficulty breathing is often the only sign a heart attack) Miss Walker was devastated.

She disliked her mother. She had been very close to her father who had died when she was about 15. He was in his 40s at the time and had died suddenly of a heart attack. Shortly after he died, she ran off to

California with her girlfriend. Her boyfriend's sudden death had been like a replay of her beloved father's death.

At the time that I first saw her, she was working at a corrections facility. While there, she had left her purse unattended and as a result, her money was stolen. The same thing happened a number of times during the course of her therapy. I never got a chance to analyze this trait. I still don't know what purposefully leaving herself vulnerable meant - maybe that she hoped to prove the existence of good in people.

Very soon I got the feeling that she was fabricating stories. Finally, I caught her in one and confronted her with the facts. Her reaction was to break down crying and confessing that she had been a prostitute when she was younger. I told her that I didn't think any less of her because of this, which seemed to cement our relationship. Nevertheless, much of what she told me through the years after that was also, in my mind, of dubious veracity.

For example, while working as a prostitute, she told me that she was protected by the mafia and often spoke of how friendly she was with the mob. She told me that while working as a prostitute she saved a great deal of money with which she bought properties in Montreal, New York City, and Cambridge, MA. She had a sister and brother-in-law, but once when I felt I needed to call them, they never returned my call. Eventually she told me she had breast cancer. I never knew whether this was true either. She said she was being treated with chemotherapy, but she never lost her hair, nor did she lose much weight, nor did she mention taking Tamoxifen. When she spoke of being cared for at a hospital in the suburbs, I asked who her doctor was. She gave me a name, but when I called the hospital to ask whether he was on the staff there, they said there was no-one there by that name. Furthermore, there was no doctor by that name in the Physicians Directory for the whole state.

She always called me the night before an appointment to remind me that she was coming. And she always paid me in cash at each visit, so I was unable to see her home address on checks.

Finally she said the prognosis of her cancer was bad and she mentioned metastases in her hip. After that she began telling me about selling all her properties. She told me that she had written a will leaving all her money to me. I told her she should leave it to her sister or some friends. However, she insisted that all her friends had either died or had let her down so that they were no longer friends, and added that her sister and brother-in-law had enough money. She said the lawyer would get in touch with me when she died.

Then one day, as usual, she called me to tell me that she would be coming in for her appointment the next morning,. The next morning she didn't show up nor did she answer her telephone. I looked in the obituaries for her name and indeed her name was listed, with her middle initial to confirm that it was her. I never heard from Miss Walker's lawyer (I never knew his name) and never heard anything about her leaving me any money. I had decided beforehand that I couldn't accept any money as I felt it would have been unethical to do so. She spoke of a charity to which she had left some money, which I would have told the lawyer to give the money to, but it never came about.

It was a strange feeling to think that I really couldn't believe what she was telling me throughout our sessions. Apparently she was trying to entertain me and herself with fantasies, although here and there it seemed to be interspersed with facts. I often wondered how I was being of any help to her. I guess she dealt with her depression this way, taking me along on her fantasies. I had had another patient who avoided dealing with an unpleasant truth in a similar way. Maybe denial can be the best defense.

#8

Mr. Connelly was in his 30s when I first saw him. He was in the midst of trying to win full custody of his children. His ex had shown little interest in the children, and she had a history of dating men who had been incarcerated. He eventually did win full custody of the children and, while young, they always showed a reluctance about visiting their mother.

The main reason Mr. Connelly came to see me was that he was afraid that he would end up in a mental hospital. He displayed no signs of severe mental illness, although, his childhood had been horrific. This was due mainly to his father. For example, when he was young and his mother was in the hospital to deliver a baby, he asked his father where his mother was. His father pointed to a piece of steak on the kitchen table saying, "There she is". A number of times, he saw his father strangling his mother or threatening to shoot her with his pistol. He actually did fire the pistol at times when he was angry, and he was frequently being arrested and put in jail. Mr. Connelly told of walking down the street towards his father who was coming from the opposite direction, and his father wouldn't even acknowledge his existence, as they passed. To punish Mr. Connelly even for minor infractions, his father would confine him to his room for a month. When Mr. Connelly was 15 years old, he got into a fist fight with his father, beating his father. His father never dared to punish Mr. Connelly or express anger at him again after that !

He related a dream to me in one of the therapy sessions where he was at the top of a hill enjoying the view of the city of Boston in the distance, when he became aware of a frightening black figure in back of him coming after him. We didn't need to guess who this figure represented.

Mr. Connelly was always there for his mother. He was the one who took her to the doctor up to the time when she was in her 90s. Mr. Connelly also took good care of his children; I recall how he took pains to impress on his son the danger of driving while under the influence of alcohol, once taking the keys to the car away from him.

Mr. Connelly needed the therapy for many years in order to feel that he could maintain his sanity. He was very considerate regarding appointments, being on time, etc. When in his middle 50s he told me that they had found something on the X-rays of his lungs. Shortly thereafter, I stopped hearing from him. When I telephoned and left messages, I never heard back. He had never expressed any suicidal intentions and he certainly would not have abandoned his mother or children, so I assumed that he went into the hospital and died. But I never got to know. It is generally considered to be an invasion of one's patient's privacy to seek follow up too assiduously.

Some people have expressed the wish to hear what it was like listening to so many different patients with all kinds of problems. I will present this section as my answers to questions I think people might ask.

What did it feel like when someone came in with a problem, for example, saying they were depressed?

I always felt it was like entering a dark cave with the patient, and without having a flashlight, feeling for clues which might lead us to the cause of the symptom. Knowing the cause would suggest how to eradicate the symptom. It was like being a detective.

Did you ever get bored listening to patients?

I rarely found myself getting bored. I do recall being bored listening to one elderly lady who constantly talked about her bowels. And some patients made me ask myself, "Is this person ever going to get better?" I often had to remind myself that sometimes it took a long time.

How did you deal with depressed patients when you were depressed yourself?

Of course, their problems came first, but once when I was depressed myself, while listening to a depressed patient, I thought, "Let me tell you about how bad I'm feeling".

How did you feel when a patient reached an insight into their problem?

Though I didn't say it, I felt like Little Jack Horner eating a pie when he put in his thumb and pulled out a plum and said, "What a good boy am I?'

I imagine some patients told you how much you helped them. How did you feel about that?

Just for one example, at the conclusion of therapy, one lady whom I had been seeing for many years, said to me, "You helped me become the woman I wanted to be !" I felt proud and felt I could tell myself that I was a pretty good psychiatrist.

People often say that therapists don't do anything but sit there and listen. What's your response to that?

Many's the time I asked myself whether I was really doing anything. Often I felt like I was the wizard of Oz, namely, a little guy behind a curtain who really didn't have any particular knowledge at all. However, in contrast to how I felt, patients often put me in an exalted position. One lady, just as we were getting up to leave our final session, looked at me and said, as if surprised, "All this time I thought you were a tall giant, but now I see that you are really no taller than I am".

How did you feel when people spoke of graphic sexual details?

That depended upon the particular patient and their situation. After some time, I reached the conclusion that anything you could imagine people doing, someone somewhere was doing just that. Some things patients said were funny. One man who was going through a divorce said, "When I first was married, I didn't care too much for cunnilingus, but after a while, I developed a taste for it". And a lady said about sex with her husband, "In fantasy it is fine, but in reality the problem becomes too big to handle". Another lady said, "If my husband were kinder to me, I'd be able to have an organism." As it was, she had 5 organisms, who were already grown up.

Was being attracted to a patient ever a problem for you?

Not really, except maybe for one young lady whom I found to be so attractive that sitting across from her caused me to constantly think about how much I desired her, probably to the point that it distracted me from working on her problem. She didn't stay with me for very long and rightly so, as I probably wasn't helping her.

How did you feel when a patient was angry with you?

I asked myself whether their anger was justified and if so, I would admit that I said something wrong. If I didn't feel it was justified, I just listened. I avoided becoming defensive, and indeed, I found that if patients felt they were allowed to express anger at me, they usually felt a lot better and were able to make more rapid progress. Being able to let anger out seemed to be curative. One young man would periodically say, "Fuck this shit" and he would get up and walk out before the time was up. To my surprise, he would always return for the next appointment.

Were there any patients you genuinely disliked?

Only one. I was seeing a couple. The man had had heart bypass surgery and his wife was constantly telling him he shouldn't do this and he shouldn't do that because he had to think of his heart. Listening to that would cause him to roll his eyes. I felt that her nagging him was probably driving him into another heart attack, doing so in the guise of intending to help him.

Talking about that, did you do couple's therapy, and how did you feel about that?

For many years, I felt incapable of treating couples. However, early in my practice, I had a successful case. A recently married couple came in, the woman complaining that she couldn't reach orgasm with sex. I asked a few questions and quickly it came out that each of them was waiting for the other one to come first. So I advised them to just think of their own pleasure and not to wait for the other one. The next appointment, just after they arrived, she announced, "Guess what? The big O".

Were there any patients who scared you?

Yes, one very big young man who had once punched his psychiatrist. He was seeing a social worker together with his mother for therapy, when he smashed a glass on his mother's head. I was just doing the prescribing, but I felt I couldn't treat him because I wasn't in control of the therapy. And he frightened me to the point where I felt compelled to give him the medications he asked for, or else. So I terminated my involvement with him.

How did you deal with patients giving you gifts?

If they were small gifts, I accepted them. I felt that trying to analyze their gift giving would be rejecting their good feelings. However, one lady wanted to buy me a Camel Hair Overcoat. I told her I couldn't accept that.

Did you often analyze dreams?

Patients didn't often bring dreams in to the sessions. Usually when they did, the symbolic meaning was so obvious I didn't have to analyze it. So, I think both us saw the dreams simply as symbolic expressions of what they were feeling.

Did you share your own stories with patients?

If I thought it might be helpful, I did. One lady came to see me because she could not get over the death of her dog. After some time listening to her grieving, I told her how I got over grieving the death of my father. I had been very close with my father. After he died, I didn't want to really enjoy anything, because I felt that if I enjoyed something, it meant that I was forgetting my father and I never wanted to forget my father. Then one day my therapist said, "You don't want to let your father go". I pictured myself holding onto my father's spirit. I thought to myself, "My father is dead and if his spirit wants to go, I shouldn't be selfish and I should let him go". After that I began to enjoy the sky, the trees, the birds, etc. and I saw that I would never forget my father even if I enjoyed life. I told my patient this story and some time later my patient let me know that I had helped her to let go of her dog's spirit.

Why did you choose to become a psychiatrist?

I wanted to find out what made people tick. I also often answered this question by saying that I was nosey. I was always very curious about people.

Finally, regarding your original desire to find out what made people tick, did you find out? And if so, what did you learn?

People's motivations are so varied that there is no simple answer to that question. But I feel that I learned to be much more tolerant and understanding of people in general. This, in turn, afforded me much more peace of mind in my everyday dealings with my fellow human beings. Reevaluating, I have to conclude that this is what I really wanted.